READY, SET, GAME!

ARCADE GAMING

BY BETSY RATHBURN

TORQUE™

BELLWETHER MEDIA • MINNEAPOLIS, MN

TORQUE brims with excitement perfect for thrill-seekers of all kinds. Discover daring survival skills, explore uncharted worlds, and marvel at mighty engines and extreme sports. In *Torque* books, anything can happen. Are you ready?

This edition first published in 2021 by Bellwether Media, Inc.

Library of Congress Cataloging-in-Publication Data

LC record for Arcade Gaming available at https://lccn.loc.gov/2020048057

Editor: Elizabeth Neuenfeldt   Designer: Brittany McIntosh

Printed in the United States of America, North Mankato, MN.

TABLE OF CONTENTS

DANCE MACHINE

Time to dance! Upbeat music plays as arrows scroll up the screen. Your feet speed across the dance pad. You are on a **combo** streak in *Dance Dance Revolution*!

As the song ends, you add more quarters to the **cabinet**. The screen lights up with arrows again. This popular arcade game is one of your favorites!

FEEL THE RHTHYM

Dance Dance Revolution is a rhythm game. It was first made in 1998. Players must time their movements to music to get a high score!

ARCADE GAMING HISTORY

The earliest arcade games were **mechanical** games made without electricity. Many were coin-operated. They were usually found at fairs and amusement parks.

New technology led to more advanced games. In 1936, the *Seeberg Ray-O-Lite* was the first arcade game to use a **light gun**. It shot a beam of light to knock down targets!

Baffle Ball

PINBALL

Pinball was one of the earliest mechanical games. *Baffle Ball* was among the first coin-operated pinball machines.

One of the first electronic arcade games was *Computer Space*. It was created by Nolan Bushnell in 1971. It had simple **graphics**. Players pressed buttons to control a rocket.

In 1975, *Gun Fight* was the first arcade game to use a **microprocessor**. This led to better graphics. Later, **vector graphics** were introduced in the 1977 game *Space Wars*.

PONG

Pong was released in 1972. It was the first video game that made money. A cabinet could make $40 per day. By 1974, there were at least 8,000 *Pong* cabinets!

ARCADE CABINETS THROUGH TIME

1936

Seeberg Ray-O-Lite

1971

Computer Space

1971

Galaxy Game

1980

Pac-Man

1981

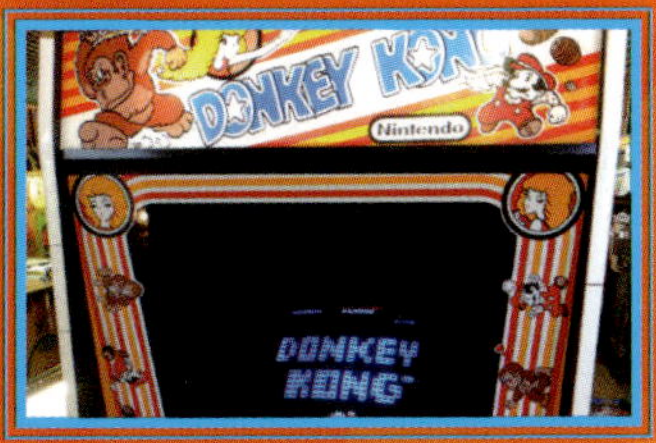

Donkey Kong

1983

Star Wars

ARCADE GAMING TIMELINE

1931

Baffle Ball, an early mechanical pinball game, is released

1971

Computer Space is one of the first electronic arcade games

1972

Pong is released, becoming the first popular arcade game

1975

Gun Fight is the first arcade game to use a microprocessor

1977

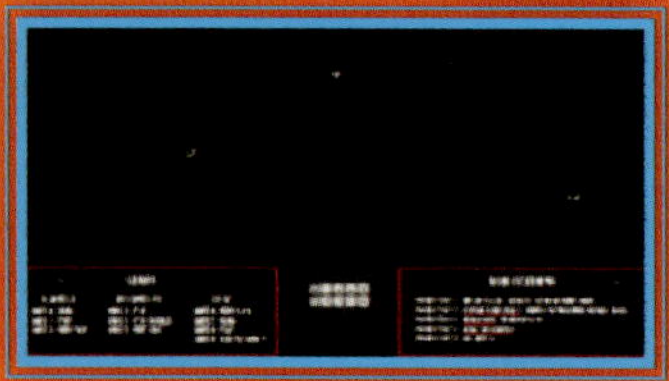

Vector graphics are introduced in *Space Wars*

1980

Pac-Man is one of the first games to include a cutscene

1991

Street Fighter II becomes one of the most popular arcade fighting games

As graphics improved, so did storytelling. Many games began using **cutscenes** in the 1980s. *Pac-Man* and *Donkey Kong* were among the most popular.

Arcades were also filled with fighting games. The Street Fighter series led the way for modern fighting games. Many players still love to play *Street Fighter II* today!

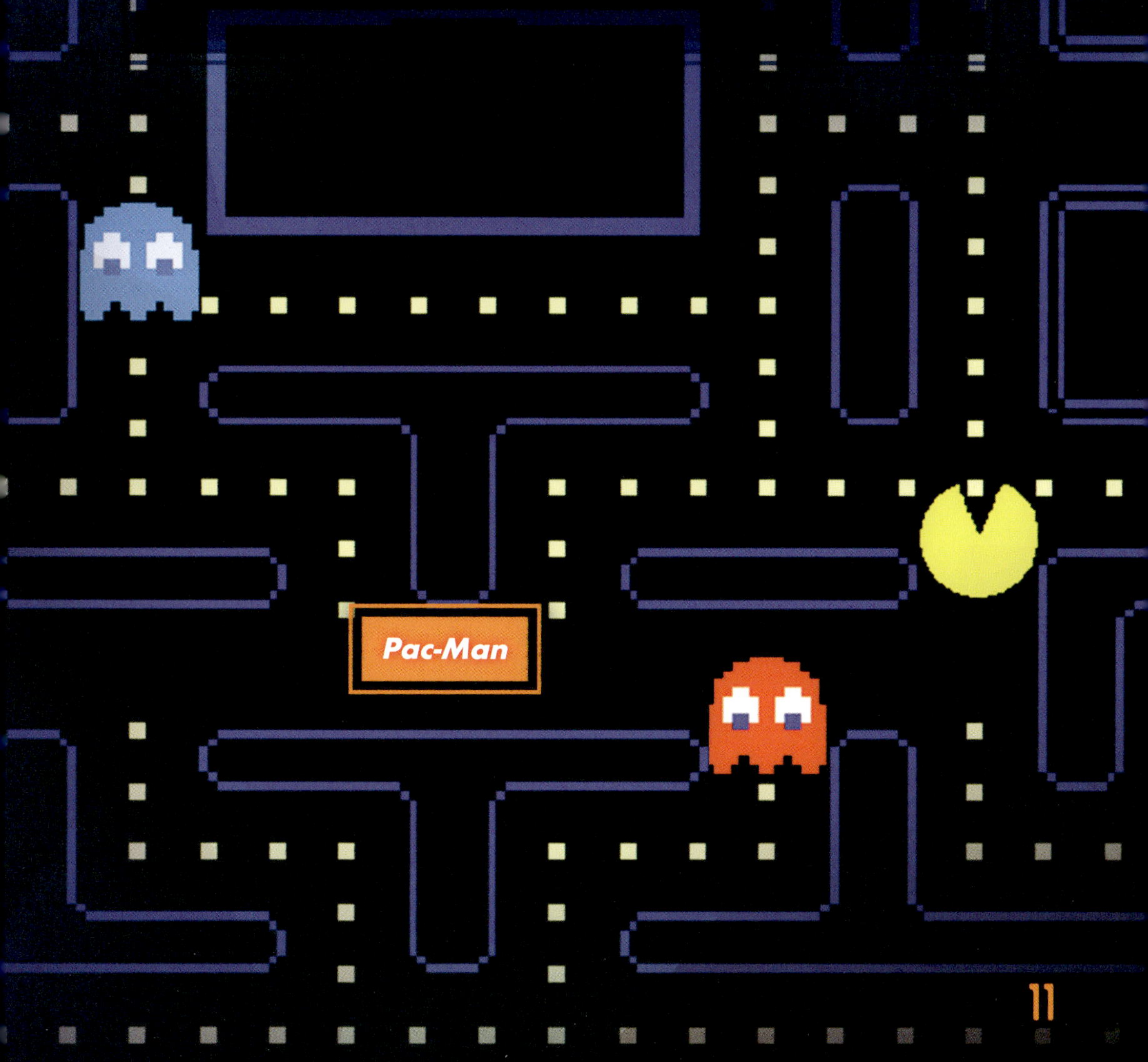

Pac-Man

ARCADE GAMING TODAY

Arcades are not as common as they once were. But many gamers still enjoy them. New technology has given some games more features. In 2001, *Virtua Fighter 4* was the first arcade game that could go online!

Despite technology, most modern arcade cabinets look like past games. Cabinets house **hardware**. Players control games with buttons and joysticks.

POPULAR ARCADE GAMES

(BY NUMBER OF CABINETS SOLD)

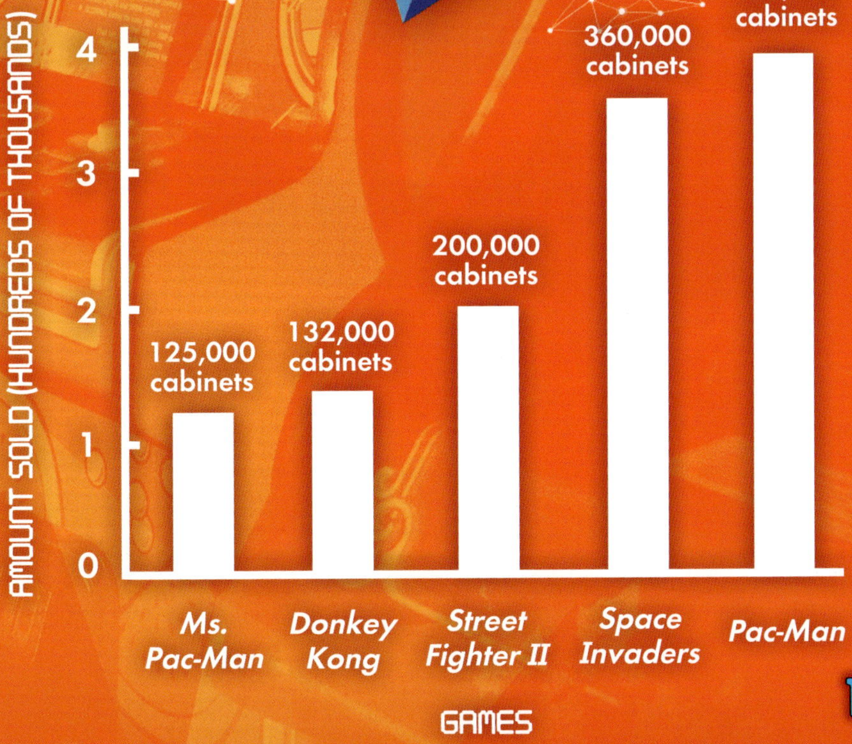

Some games have special hardware. Flying or driving games often have special seats. Players may use a steering wheel and pedals. Large screens make the games feel real!

Virtual reality arcades are also growing. Gamers wear a **headset** and use controllers to explore a new world!

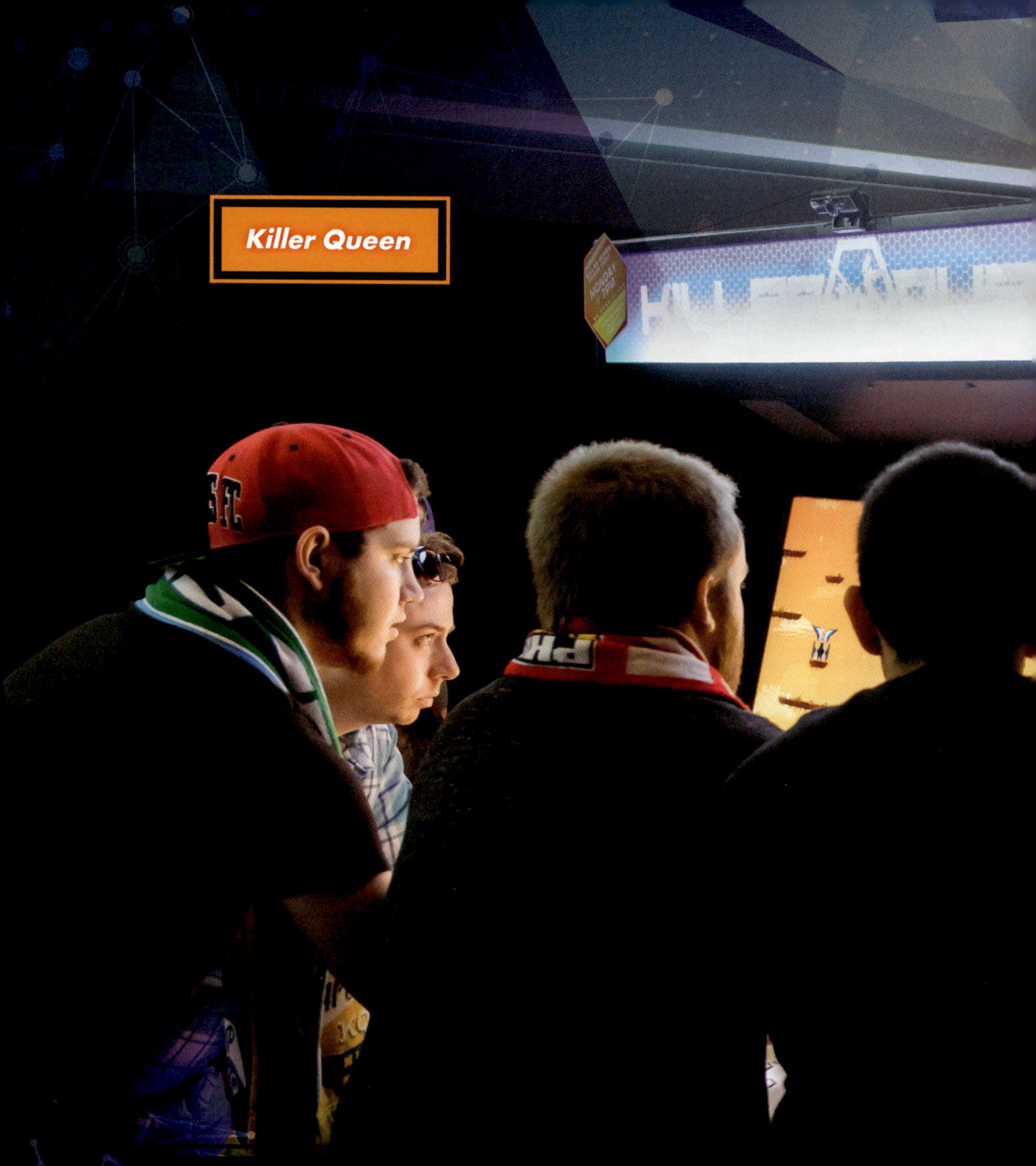

Killer Queen

Game makers are also introducing new styles of play to arcade games. The 2013 **strategy game** *Killer Queen* has a big following.

Unlike many arcade games, *Killer Queen* is made for 10 players. Players work together on teams to complete tasks. Games like this may make arcades more popular in the future!

GAME SPOTLIGHT

GAME *Killer Queen*

YEAR 2013

TYPE strategy

DESCRIPTION Teams of five work together to defeat the other team. Worker bees may collect 12 berries or ride a snail to the finish line to win. But they must protect their queen bee. If the queen is defeated three times, the other team wins!

There are still thousands of arcades around the world. People visit to play at their favorite cabinets. The best players may get on the high score table!

Star Wars: Battle Pod

Many games are designed after popular movies or music. *Star Wars: Battle Pod* lets gamers shoot down TIE fighters in a galaxy far away. Pinball machines have featured Marvel characters.

THE ARCADE GAMING COMMUNITY

There are many arcade gaming events around the world. Fans of older games still play head-to-head in *Donkey Kong* and *Street Fighter II*.

Some gamers join **leagues**. They gather at arcades to meet friends and play their favorite games. In the arcade gaming community, there is always someone to play with!

ARCADE GAMING EVENT SPOTLIGHT

EVENT IFPA World Pinball Championship

HOST International Flipper Pinball Association

GAME pinball

WHEN IT HAPPENS once per year

WHERE IT HAPPENS around the world

RECENT CHAMPIONS Johannes Ostermeier (2019), Raymond Davidson (2018)

GLOSSARY

cabinet—the structure surrounding the computer and other hardware that make up an arcade game

combo—a series of moves or tricks played back-to-back that result in a higher score

cutscenes—parts of a game where the player has no control of the character; cutscenes are like short movies.

graphics—images displayed on a computer screen

hardware—physical pieces of computers or other technology

headset—a helmet, visor, or other item that a person wears on their head to experience virtual reality

leagues—groups that come together to compete at a certain activity

light gun—a device that shoots a laser at objects or graphics on the screen

mechanical—related to machines; mechanical games have no electronic parts.

microprocessor—a small chip that holds a computer's memory

strategy game—a game that requires careful planning to achieve goals

vector graphics—graphics created with sequences of commands or math equations

virtual reality—related to games that allow players to explore a human-made setting

TO LEARN MORE

AT THE LIBRARY

Gregory, Josh. *History of Esports.* Ann Arbor, Mich.: Cherry Lake Publishing, 2020.

Hansen, Dustin. *Game On!: Video Game History from Pong and Pac-Man to Mario, Minecraft, and More.* New York, N.Y.: Feiwel & Friends, 2016.

Rathburn, Betsy. *Computer Gaming.* Minneapolis, Minn.: Bellwether Media, 2021.

ON THE WEB

FACTSURFER

Factsurfer.com gives you a safe, fun way to find more information.

1. Go to www.factsurfer.com.

2. Enter "arcade gaming" into the search box and click 🔍.

3. Select your book cover to see a list of related content.

INDEX

The images in this book are reproduced through the courtesy of: BPH, front cover; Stephen Chung/ Alamy, p. 4; AARON SHOWALTER/ Newscom, p. 5; FPG / Staff/ Getty Images, p. 6; SheDrivesMeCrazy/ Pinside, p. 7; Rob Boudon/ Wikipedia, p. 8; MrBigglesWorth3/ Wikipedia, p. 9 (*Seeberg Ray-O-Lite*); Staffan Vilcans/ Flickr, p. 9 (*Computer Space*); Brain Hicks/ Flickr, p. 9 (*Galaxy Game*); Alexander Podshivalov/ Dreamstime, p. 9 (*Pac-Man*); Chynna Malucelli/ Dreamstime, p. 9 (*Donkey Kong*); Rob DiCaterino/ Flickr, p. 9 (*Star Wars*); *Space Wars*/ Wikipedia, p. 10 (top); *Street Fighter II*/ Mark R Johnson, p. 10 (bottom); *Pac-Man*/ Tegan Jones, p. 11; Andrew Cline/ Alamy, pp. 12-13; Bloomberg / Contributor/ Getty Images, p. 14; Tomohiro Ohsumi / Stringer/ Getty Images, p. 15; Michael Dunn/ Flickr, pp. 16-17; *Killer Queen*/ William Cennamo/ Screen Rant, p. 17; ZUMA Press, Inc./ Alamy, pp. 18-19; Xinhua/ Alamy, pp. 20-21.